Who's calling?...

William F. Maestri

Author

Rossin

Artist

Éditions du Signe

Jesus

Cover: "**Jesus**" (detail), 2009

Frontispiece: **Monsignor Thomas Kenny**, 2009

In Memoriam

Monsignor Thomas Kenny

1939–2008

Who's calling ?...

Contents

INTRODUCTION

On October 30th of 2008, the Archdiocese of Atlanta lost one of her most beloved priests, Monsignor Tom Kenny. Forty-three years before, in 1965, a newly-ordained "Father" Kenny had arrived in Atlanta from his native Ireland. He was the youngest of 11 children, who early on discerned a vocation to the priesthood. During his studies at All Hallows Seminary, he accepted the invitation of Archbishop Paul J. Hallinan and decided to come to the United States in order to devote his life to the service of the Church in North Georgia. For more than four decades, he lived as a devoted priest, serving well the parishes where he was assigned and glorifying God through the strong character that endeared him to his brother priests and to the many friends he made during the long years of his pastoral work. For the last eighteen years of his life Monsignor Kenny was rector at the Cathedral of Christ the King.

This volume of poetry, authored and now published in loving memory of Monsignor Tom Kenny, is the work of the noted Catholic writer, Father William Maestri, a priest of the Archdiocese of New Orleans. Father Maestri composed these poems during a yearlong residence at Christ the King Parish, while enjoying on a daily basis the company and conversation of Monsignor Kenny. The imprint of this encounter was lasting. After Monsignor Kenny's death Father Maestri decided to give the Cathedral Parish his poetic meditations on readings from the New Testament as a tribute to his friend.

Monsignor Kenny's presence is sorely missed by those who knew him as he never let the opportunity for a friendly encounter pass by. He leaves behind countless friends. He is missed especially by his brother priests, who enjoyed his warm sociability and often depended on the firm strength of his advice and guidance. Thanks be to God for our belief in the Communion of Saints – for that is certainly where this man of Faith will await reunion with all who loved him and called him "Father" and friend. May this volume, conceived in friendship and dedicated to Monsignor Kenny's memory, serve now as a reminder to pray for the repose of his soul.

✠ **Wilton D. Gregory,**
Archbishop of Atlanta

CATHEDRAL *of* CHRIST THE KING

PREFACE

Monsignor Thomas Kenny inspired the devotion of priests and parishioners which has led to many gifts to honor his memory. The most unique is the gift of this book of poems by Rev. William F. Maestri, who composed them during his residency in Atlanta in 2008-09. He gave the rights to them to the Cathedral of Christ the King in Atlanta, Georgia in Monsignor's honor.

The proceeds from the sale of this book benefit the Monsignor Kenny Memorial Fund, dedicated to assisting poor and homeless people and to nurturing and sustaining vocations to the priesthood – a vocation that shaped and fulfilled Fr. Kenny's life for more than 50 years when he first entered the seminary in Dublin, Ireland in 1958.

We are indebted to Fr. Maestri, Rossin, and all those who have worked to make this book a worthy memorial to a pastor held dear by people far beyond the reach of the Cathedral parish.

Rev. Francis G. McNamee
Pastor of the Cathedral

AUTHOR'S NOTE

The initial excitement of coming to Atlanta and teaching at the John Marshall Law School was quickly replaced by the urgent need to find a place to stay. To be at once employed and homeless left me, well, unsettled on many levels.

At first blush being a priest in need of residence strikes one as no large task. Within the Archdiocese there are many mansions, I mean rectories and religious houses, to hang my hat. Not so fast. It is risky business for the one seeking an abode and equally risky for the one who invites you to stay. Not all marriages work; nor do all living arrangements. And divorce can be quite messy.

Being a creature of habit (perhaps it would be better for me to say a creature of ritual) I turned to the method I have used in the past. Armed with the National Catholic Directory, I turned to the section dealing with the Atlanta Archdiocese (this method is grounded in Scripture, "seek and ye shall find.")

The first entry is appropriately enough, the Cathedral of Christ the King. My initial reaction was, "fat chance." Unfortunately being more Augustinian (pessimistic) than Franciscan (hopeful) I immediately dismissed the notion of being offered a place at the Cathedral. The rectory was probably crawling with high-church types with incense constantly surrounding them. Not a good fit.

For some reason, I couldn't shake the idea of calling the Cathedral. Label it curiosity, a perverse sense of humor, or the prideful need to have suspicions confirmed (I quickly came to see it as God's grace to one of His skeptical children from the Crescent City), I dialed the Cathedral.

The National Catholic Directory indicated that one Monsignor Thomas Kenny was the Rector (Pastor). I knew what to expect – a high-sounding ecclesiastic type who was going to say "no way" but wrap it in the sugary church-speak so rejection would be easier to swallow.

My initial conversation with Monsignor Kenny went as follows:

> M: "Hello, Monsignor Kenny? My name is William Maestri, a priest with the Archdiocese of New Orleans. This coming academic year I'll be teaching at the John Marshall Law School. I'm in need of a place to live while teaching. I was wondering if there might be room at the Cathedral?"

(Again I knew what the response would be – NO! In fact, my fingers were making their way down the list of possible parishes to call next.)

K: "Bill, there will be a room available in the fall and you would be more than welcome to stay."

It took a few seconds for his words to overcome my expectation. It was that simple, direct, and in the best traditions of the west of Ireland, hospitable. While my expectations proved once again to be terribly wrong, my initial measure of the man was not. In fact, over the all too few short months I got to know Monsignor Kenny, my appreciation of the man and Catholic priest only grew.

I need not enlarge Monsignor Kenny in death more than he was in life. From what I was blessed to observe, he was a good man who loved Jesus, the Church, his vocation, and the people God entrusted to his care. Pray that such may be said of us: we were faithful in our duty to God, loving to those around us; and dedicated to a work beyond satisfying our own wants.

I found out that Monsignor loved poetry; not surprising for an Irishman. This volume of poems, based on the New Testament, is offered with utmost respect and gratitude to his memory. I am sure I speak for the countless souls touched by this grace-filled priest when I say I am a better man, disciple of Jesus, and priest for having known Monsignor Kenny.

Heaven's gain is ours as well, for I am sure that Monsignor continues to be prayerfully mindful of our pilgrimage towards home. Until that blessed day of reunion, may we continue to honor Monsignor Kenny's memory by the way we live the gift of each day.

This volume of poems is enriched with an introduction by Archbishop Gregory, and the current Pastor of the Cathedral, Reverend Francis McNamee. Both have made this stranger welcome. Both are gratefully remembered in prayer.

Finally, I am grateful to the dedicated staff of the Cathedral of Christ the King who took their valuable time to make this project a reality. A special word of appreciation is extended to Margaret Jones, who organized the overall production. Katherine Boshinski, who skillfully typed the handwritten (!) manuscript. Rossin, artist, lent his professional expertise for the final product. Each made valuable contributions so this work would be a fitting tribute to Monsignor Kenny.

William F. Maestri

William F. Maestri
March 17, 2009
Feast of Saint Patrick

xi

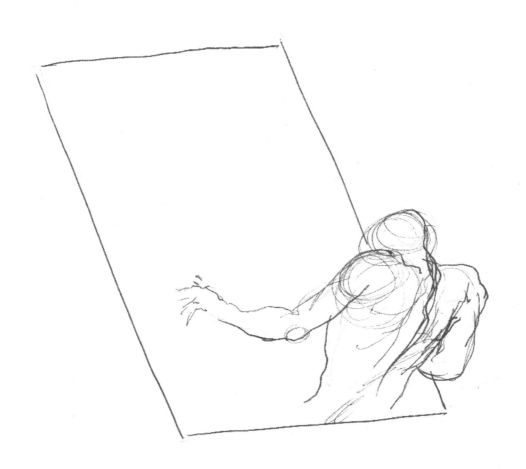

the call

the call

I dreamed a phone ring in the night,
    even one that comes with dawn's first light.
So jarring and abrupt,
    I can't help but to jump up.
Shake off sleep, not quite awake;
    caught between velvet night and morning's break.
I offer a weary "hello", waiting for a voice I know,
    knowing good news comes at a different pace;
        from another place.
Finally the words, "Follow Me."
    What can this be? A nut? A joke?

        A wrong number to disturb my slumber?
After this I can't rest or sleep; there is no peace.
    The sun now is rising in the east,
        time to face the world with its beasts.

The day long past, I did my best, now to rest.
    Sleep won't come, those morning words abide,
        I find no place to hide.
A pill, a drink, yet still I think, "Follow Me."
    What is the link? My eyes to blink.
Just let me be. I refuse to see.

Matthew 4:18-22, p. 55

wake up!

wake up!

Up and at 'em, the American way;
    another day, come what may;
        earn my pay; have my say.

Out the door; fight the war;
    even the score.
Tough world; not for girlie girls;
    cut throat; enjoy and gloat.
        Cry in your beer; the only cheer.
Up and down, in a world of clowns...

Through the door...slow...,
    a glimmer; a place unfamiliar.
        In a space and time not mine.
          All is left behind.

How strange I feel; what's the deal?
    Computer; cell phone; grey canyons
        gone like air...but where? Scared.

Must be a dream,
    a rival's scheme.
        I'll wake up.
          Don't scream.

All once mine up in smoke;
    a distant shore moving close.
        Standing still, I feel a chill;
          a Stranger, a Ghost.

Mark 1:16-20, p. 55

surrender

surrender

I fought to shake it off,
    all my efforts were for naught.
Full days with empty nets,
    my best I did to cover bets.

No longer. I feel a hunger stronger.
    A strange attraction; a call to action.
I'm used to risk; I know the tricks.
    Not a bargain made; no mention of a waiting grave.

Power, riches, and such things would give
    to heart a cause to sing.
Yet now they sound a noisy gong,
    my soul no longer to belong;
        only to the One who came into my night
            with an invite, "Follow me. Come and see."

I desire to say yes, to give my all, to do my best.
    I know the cost, so much is lost.
        Where the gain amidst the pain; clearing after rain;
        the splendor with surrender?

So much unknown, my soul does groan,
    to know the way before I stay;
        guarantees before I cast my lot with Thee.

John 1:35-51, p. 56

15

homecoming

homecoming

Quit while you're ahead, learn to put things to bed.
 Cut losses; count gains; no need for pain.
 Speak their language, stroke the flames; enjoy the game.

What's wrong with playing to the crowd?
 How sweet the words sung aloud,
"He's one of us. He's done good; no longer works with wood."
 He's come home, this one local grown,
 to touch hearts of stone.

What! To us dare preach? Beyond your reach.
 Get out of town; do it now.
Don't leave alone. Take your followers as you go,
 make it quick, dare not slow.

The verdict clear: you've changed; not the same.
 Feel the shame.
 What's your game?
 We're not to blame.
 Things are not the same.

Mark 6:1-6, p. 57

bad company

bad company | The company you keep reveals who you are, want to be,
and what you seek; speaks about your needs; more so
your greeds.

What's He up to? Not a clue; came out the blue. He knew.
Not me. I never see.
What I know this one's not one of us. Wrong occupation;
taxation. Heavy burdens on our backs just to fill
his sacks.
Take it back, don't let him come; this scum.
Too late. He leaves his station; now in our congregation.

Fine. Let him fall behind, lose his way, go astray.
I didn't call; just let him fall; watch the bouncing ball.
See if I stop or bend; I'm not a friend.
Not me. Leave me be. He's on his own. Deaf to groans.
Let's keep it straight through narrow gate. Another chose
you, I know not why, another castle in the sky.

Matthew 9:9-13, p. 57

suspicion

suspicion

A tax collector among us,
    now one named Judas,
        no wonder no one wants us.
This keeper of the trust,
    driven by lust, for his own august.
He cares not for the widow; orphan; poor
    he ignores.
Silver, gold he wants to hoard,
    his only goal is gold and more.
Grasping, clasping, purse held tight,
    not for right but money's might.

Can't shake the feeling; unappealing;
    downright appalling; thoughts a-reeling.
This bad one called will cause a fall;
    beckoning yields a reckoning.

Wonder if He suspects; maybe regrets?
    No looking back, no time for that.
        Away He goes.
            Let it close.

To lie down is my one desire; warm by the fire.
    Rest my head on any bed; the ground a familiar spread.
        Here's some space; I know the place; full of grace.

Mark 3:13-19, p. 58

wedding

wedding

Now you're talking, not just walking.
    To a wedding we're a-heading.
Up to Cana, Galilee; the invite includes me.
      Put on a shine; don't waste time; clocks a runnin' on my dime;
      others drinkin' my red wine.

Good food, good drink, enough for all; at last a ball.
    What? We're out of drink; gone in a blink; this stinks.
Well, time to go; ready to blow. No use hanging 'round this town;
    no more time for clowns.

Water into wine; what's His trick? He's so slick!
    The best for last; time long past; guests aghast.
      Why the choicest last?
I don't care, just want my fill; even some to spill.
    This new wine cheers the heart; no clouds to thoughts.
      What has He wrought?

Time to go; take it slow.
    One more for the road; add to my heavy load.
      To lie down now is my one desire; the glow of a fire.
        In my bed with spinning head; thoughts of dread;
      what lies ahead?
      I do not know but I will go,
        I will follow where He leads,
          no life of easy; let me sleep – please!

John 2:1-12, p. 58

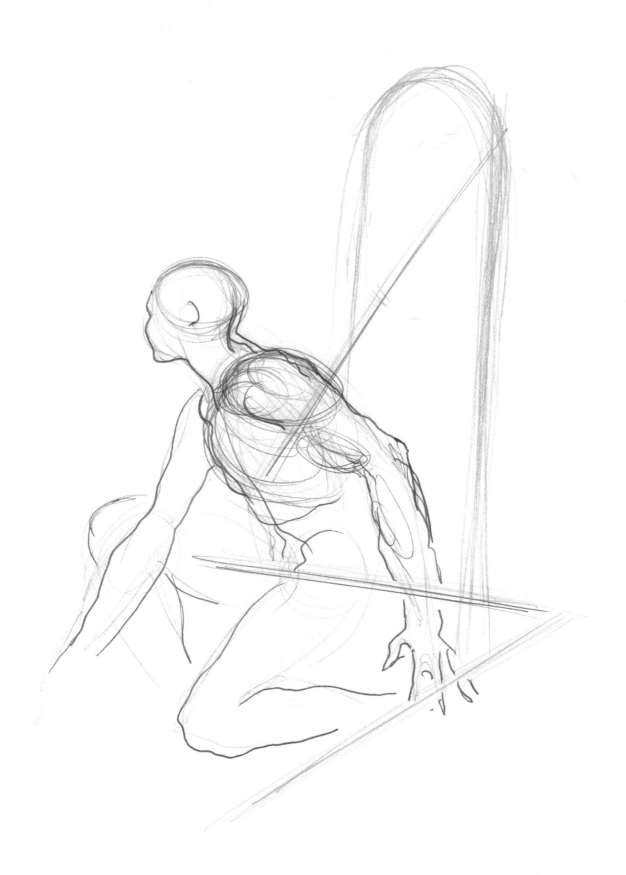

temple

temple

Can't stand prosperity or good reviews;
    He just wants bad news.
Confrontation; teach a lesson; a sign to the blind.

From wedding now to Temple cleansing; money changers
    why the anger?
        No big deal; let's keep it real.
            Keep your cool; don't play the fool.

Worship needs its sacrifices;
    God desires; the Law requires;
        obeying demands paying.

From His mouth comes a shout, "Temple down
    to the ground. In three days' time; restoration,
        resurrection; celebration."
           Fail to see the connection.

Surprise! Some come to His side.
    He's still not satisfied.
        Enthusiasm soon runs dry.
           What's he want, the sky?
               Just want to run and hide.

John 2:13-25, p. 59

the end?

the end?

Each day filled with ire; soul on fire;
　　by water to confront established order.
Claims to be sent; his call to repent.
　　A voice in the wilderness; ear now hear;
　　　　His time is near; hearts convert, not too late.

Anger thunders from the throne; power will have its hour.
　　No more of him; this baptizer, rabble-rouser;
　　　　Returned to normalcy, just how it should be.

Followers will seek another to offer hope;
　　an opium for their pain; numb the brain.
　　　　What have they gained?

This Other One who comes after, stranger still,
　　He too I must kill.
　　　　Not enough to end His life;
　　　　　　what disturbs are His words.
　　　　　　　　How to eliminate requires more than hate;
　　　　　　　　　　a weakness within, will be this end.

Luke 3:1-20, p. 59

identity

identity

Once again on the move;
    hard for me to get my groove.
        What's He out to prove?

Surprise. A doubt revealed amidst the zeal;
    wants to know the latest gossip;
        not events but about Himself.

"Who do people say I am?" Comes the opinions of the minions:
    "John the Baptist, Elijah, Jeremiah, one of the prophets"; a hot topic.
        None correct, I suspect. I'll be candid, cause for slander,
    "You are the Christ, Son of God." That wasn't hard;
        came easy, kind of breezy, a Dove from above.
    Gave me praise. He was pleased; even offered keys,
        My authority for all to see.

Didn't last, I had to gasp. He called me Satan; an obstacle,
    just wanted to keep Him from a place called Skull.
        He's so fickle, I'm in a pickle.
            Worst of all He starts again, about lesson way back when;
            self-denial, cross, death, and all the rest.

Somber silence. Apprehension. Cut the tension; an explanation.
    No use. No more abuse.
        Tabor just ahead.
            What's in store; what more?

Matthew 16:13-20, p. 61

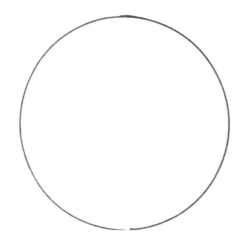

dis(trans)figuration

dis(trans)figuration

Tabor, a safe harbor. Make things right, even the score,
said that before.
To the top; air is thin; day so hot; I might drop.
Keys useless; don't fit His lock.

What's going on? He's transformed; face like the sun;
clothes white as light; can't be right.
He must have stroke; knows the right folk.
Conversing with Moses and Elijah; Jesus glad
I'm here beside ya'.

From a cloud a voice clear and loud, "My beloved Son
hear him now."
Afraid, want out of this parade, no part of His charade.

Can't move. Holding fast to the ground, another sound;
a familiar voice, "be not afraid."
Looking up; He's by himself; no one else.

Heading down the mountain one command, "tell the vision
to no man." Why not? This is hot. This stuff
would silence all the guff and scuttle-butt.

He won't go along; sings his own song, "Disfiguration before
Transformation."
Suffering, cross, and death; a familiar theme, another scene?
More confusion.
An illusion?

Matthew 17:1-8, p. 61

delay

delay

Martha confronts Him with words to be heard:
　　"What took you so long to right the wrong?"
　　　Lazarus is dead, an untimely end,
　　　　with others' needs time he did spend.
　　"It is you who were busy with many things;
　　　in place of my brother, you chose others."

Sensing danger by words of anger, Martha shifts gears,
　　hoping He hears, not words but tears.
　　　Lazarus, His friend, can't be the end,
　　　　pray the Father the tomb be rend.
　　Jesus call out, give forth a shout;
　　　summon your friend, divine power spend.

Lazarus comes forth; bandages, bondage broken.
　　How? The power of His word spoken.
　　　The one held dear is returned to life
　　　　by He who is Life and Light.

All filled with awe and gratitude
　　of this display of Divine plentitude.
　　　But not all are pleased or deeply impressed;
　　　　a plot must be hatched with dispatch.
　　　　　Crowds have a way of getting out of control;
　　　　　　must strengthen our hold.
　　　　　　Do all we can,
　　　　　　　to keep Him from Jerusalem.

Perhaps the solution lies within,
　　to that group of disciples;
　　　Maybe one is without scruples.
　　A bag of silver is worth the cost.
　　　Hurry, before all is lost!

John 11:1-44, p. 62

the crowd

the crowd

Here we are in Jerusalem; will not end well for Him.
The crowds with all their songs and hymns,
dances, dirges, will give way to scourges.

Fickle crowd with their Hosannas loud;
give them time, they'll change their tune;
come around; "crucify Him" their new refrain; play the game.

Whatever happens, can't blame me, long ago tried to
make Him see; not He.

Out from the crowd emerge the Pharisees; His turn for a
rebuke; a turn of the worm.
"Tell the crowd to keep silent," they demand; command.
He has an answer ready; strong and steady, "Even stones
would not be silent."
He won't relent; repent. His last chance spent.

Can't help but think what might have been; a different end;
more time to spend with true friends.
Too late for regrets, made my bed; now lay my head.
No turning back; my fate sealed; joined to
Him, can't undo the deal.
All seems unreal.

Luke 19:28-40, p. 64

\\25

an example

an example

This looks familiar; something similar; a glimmer
of Passover past.
Yet unique. It speaks a language hard to learn,
I want to spurn.
The Master is the servant; upside down;
stripes bring healing; thorns a crown;
cross a throne, glory shone.

Only words, just absurd;
Power, glory, that's the story;
meekness really weakness.

What's he doing? Washing feet; never mine;
out His mind.
Must preserve His dignity; save Him
from this absurdity.
He ups the stakes, can have no place
unless my feet He washes; proceed
I will concede.
Head, hands, and heart just the start;
all over clean.
Make me thine; heart does pine.

Example not fully grasped; the first are last.
Topsey, turvey; just plain crazy.

Talk of betrayal; no need for a trial,
I know who it is;
Judas the traitor of our Saviour.
Take him out into the night; set him straight; out of sight.
No delay; he'll get his pay.
But wait; He confounds our haste.
One more thing to do before it's through.

John 13:1-20, p. 65

morsel

morsel | We know how to deal with a spy,
a little old fashion eye for an eye.
Let this Judas die; hang himself high,
say goodbye.

Jesus gives us a look, shakes His head;
what more can be said?
Have come to know who is the betrayer;
ask the Beloved he'll discover.

What's this, the morsel dipped into the dish…
to Judas, who now leaves us.
Into the night goes the scoundrel;
this lost soul; he escapes our hold.

Wouldn't want his fate; I'll keep the faith;
to the bitter end, I'll remain a friend.
The sword is ready, I'll be steady;
come what may, He knows I'll stay.
no matter the trial; never a denial.

I'm the rock, I have the key;
He can count on me.
Watch. You'll see.

Luke 22:21-23, p. 66

John 13:21-31, p. 67

memory

memory

Came the test, would He protest?
Away in silence, no resistance.
No talk of rights; led out of sight.
Where's the crowd, so loud, with 'Hosanna'
just days ago? How soon to change their tune,
"Crucify; let Him die. Away with Him!"

Escape through that gate; increase my pace; too late.
"It's the buzz, you're one of His," she says.
"Not so; let me go."
"I saw you too, now He's through; what about you?"
"It's a mistake; give me a break.
Gotta go; it's getting late."

Hear the sound; how it hounds; inside my head,
His words resound, "you'll deny; disown;
to you I am unknown."
Bitter weep, the tears do heap; stain my cheek;
I sow; I reap.
The loathing mine to keep.

Another sound from the dark; jingle, jangle;
silver coins, bitter gain; familiar refrain.
Oh the pain!
Out of the shadow a figure known;
traitor…betrayer…denier…
We are one. Deed is done.

John 18:15-18, 25-27, p. 67

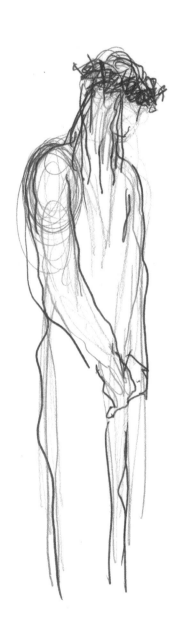

loud silence

loud silence

"Silence is not golden," said Pilate,
    arms folded.
The one in love with power,
    before the One who is Love's Power.
Pilate's hour to have his way,
    rendered weak by One who will not speak.
"I have the power to release or condemn; let's try again.
    Name the men You now defend, with a silence,
      You don't comprehend.
        No choice but to condemn."

"You have no power in this hour if not granted from above,"
    comes the reply as from on High.
"It is you who need release; true peace."
"Hear truth that liberates; drives out fear;
    replaces hate with Love so great.
      It's not too late. Come through the Gate."

"You talk of truth; what a ruse.
    Can't let you loose; too dangerous among us;
      deal with you like wind to dust,"
      declares a troubled Pilate to a
        Suffering Servant still unbent.

"Behold Man of Sorrows, where are Your powers?
    You a King? A divine sting.
Crowned with thorns; all friends are gone.

Scourged, made sport; now lose heart?
    Condemned.
      Your end.

John 18:28-40, p. 68

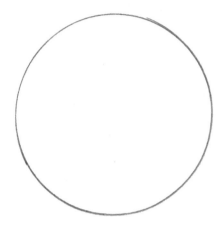

why me?

why me?

Why me?
　　　Just came to see. Northing more than curiosity.
　　　　Not too keen; I'm from Cyrene.
　　　　　Not my Cross; not my boss; not my loss.
　　　　　Feel sorry? Not mine to carry.

There must be another to share this burden;
　　lift Him up for the bitter end.
　　　Doesn't He have friends?

What's the use? Quite clear, the end is near.
　　On the way, on top a hill;
　　　in either case they will to kill.

Worse than carrying the Cross is His look;
　　so much pain, so little gain.
　　　Who is to blame? To whom the shame?

He whispers to me; saved by the crowd, so loud,
　　couldn't, wouldn't, hear the word. So afraid.

My burden near its end; never come this way again.
　　Another place my life to spend.
　　　It is finished; at an end.
Why did He whisper, "friend"?

Luke 23:26-32, p. 69

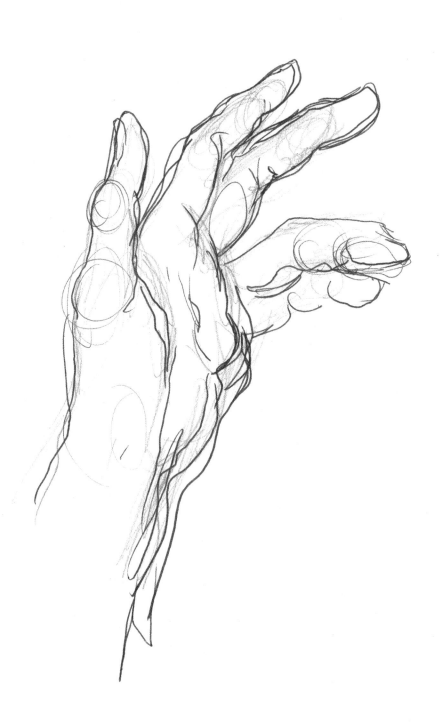

one's own

one's own

"I heard You preach; teach,"
   came the claim filled with disdain.
"Save Yourself, and us too," said the thief
   in this hour so bleak.
God's Son You claim to be
   surely not for You this tree.
      Why not set us free"
"Why doesn't Your Father take a cue;
   rescue us…You?
      Doesn't seem to have a clue."

"Be silent. Relent. We need to repent,"
   came the rebuke from another one condemned;
      wants to make amends.
         Turns to the One who heals all rends.

"Remember me when You come into Your kingdom,"
   request from one beset with burdens great;
      surrounded by much hate.

Comes the reply, so sublime,
   "You will be with Me in paradise."
      For each of us, the gift of grace;
         come in haste.
Fill my space with Your power at the
   hour of my death; give me rest.

Luke 23:33-43, p. 69

the UNusual suspects

the UNusual suspects

On a hill so still,
gone the thrill of the kill;
gone the shrill voices, filled with curses.

Yet there remain figures strange,
don't belong, just seems wrong.
Each a past filled with shame, pain;
much to hide, much to blame.
One of ill repute; one a brute.
One of lust, one of power,
joined together in this hour.

A past hidden, now forgiven;
He set things right, brought the Light, now out of sight.
Who to replace that empty space,
not to condemn but befriend, to the end?

Need a word, must be heard.
Who will speak in a place so bleak?
No trumpets blast, that's long past.
What?! A word at last.

From the rear, a source so queer.
Move near, must hear.
One with sword and spear, loud and clear:
"Truly the Son of God."

How odd.

Matthew 27:45-56, p. 70

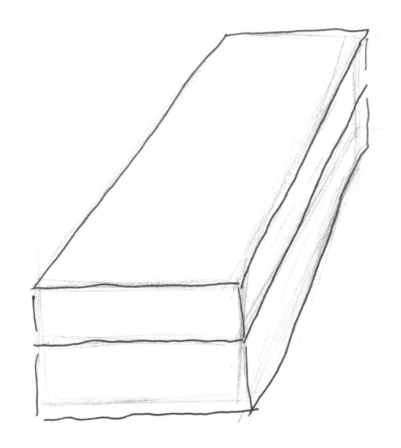

the tomb

the tomb

Tomb so silent do relent, do not hide;
  tell about the other side.
Your secrets not to share; not to spare,
  the dread our always approaching end.

Oh tomb you contain the One who bore our pain;
  for you the gain, for us the loss beyond all cost.
    We feel so lost.
Proud sepulcher you offer no succor, as you
  mock by the rock which blocks the way.
    Those within must stay.
      No more the light of day.
        Those without can only pray.

Victorious tomb you celebrate our defeat;
  only left to retreat into those places,
    cold and deep; estate of eternal sleep.

Tomb, monument to death, your power for all to see;
  no more this Man of Galilee.

Mark 15:42-47, p. 70

women

women

Women rushed from the tomb
with a story, tale of glory;
the Flower crushed now blooms;
wonder in place of gloom.

That prison could not hold the One,
God's story told. Women's voices bold:
He once dead now lives; new life to give.

Who can believe? No more to be deceived.
Left everything to follow; the earth did swallow.
Earth's verdict not reversed; sin's curse for each a place.
Reality must be faced.

What if reports are true? What to do?
Let Him rest in peace,
His death to keep; in memories
to sustain through the pain.

Head says stay, heart says go;
inner tension; apprehension; soon resolved, doubts absolved.
Feet make haste to the place of lost grace;
or disgrace.

Hope against hope – disfiguration now transfiguration?

What do we see?
Eyes behold a sight to fright;
tomb torn asunder, hearts filled with wonder.
Empty grace; trick, charade; the wrong cave.

How to explain a thing so strange?

What do you see? A mystery? A story of God's glory?
Mind confused. Will can't choose.
Afraid to lose.
Left to muse…

Luke 24:1-12, p. 71

on the road-again

on the road-again

The last three years spent on the go,
    so little to show; gone the glow.
Hopes dashed, dreams crashed,
    past events leave us aghast.

Disillusion our new companion.
    Back to the everyday of yesteryears,
    hearts filled with tears.

Who is this Stranger who walks with us?
    He wants to know our conversation;
    must be cautious, prudent hesitation.
Slow to trust, will not be rushed.
    Better yet, let's leave Him in the dust.

Yet as He speaks our pain subsides;
    He proves to be our true Guide,
    about the suffering ways of God;
    He slowly lifts the fog;
His pain for our gain; His rising enflames hearts' desire;
    be our fire.

Must hear more, make Him stay, the day has passed away.
    Share more the story of God's glory.
    Share our meal; a time to heal.

Luke 24:13-35, p. 72

doubting

doubting

He came into their midst; their fears and cares;
    His to bear.
        He did ease with words of "Peace."
Still bearing scars of Good Friday's war,
    but now transformed.
Again the word of "Peace" to tame that Roaring Beast.

Enter Thomas late to the scene.
    Words of faith find no place,
        no room for grace;
            not serene but another scene.

Nothing less than touch and probe will ease this
    load of doubt; now all about.
The One of Peace reappears with words of invitation,
    overcome your hesitation.
Place your hand within my side, let your doubt subside.
    Comes the declaration, "My Lord, my God";
        words of liberation.

Beyond this moment of doubt belief does run, to rest on
    those yet to come.
        Those who will believe not by sight,
            but by the might of faith's holy light.

John 20:24-29, p. 73

do you love me?

do you love me?

Breakfast done, more talk to come;
more change, more the same.
A question so direct, danger I detect.
"Do you love me?" comes the question.
"Of course I do"; no hesitation.

Not once but twice more the inquiry, "Do you love me?".
"You know I do"; deep frustration.
"Feed my lambs, tend my sheep", comes the instruction.
Now a prediction.

My death to His I will follow; fallow,
yet hallowed by His crucifixion.
My conviction – follow Him.
Denial gives way to affirmation.

John 21:15-19, p. 73

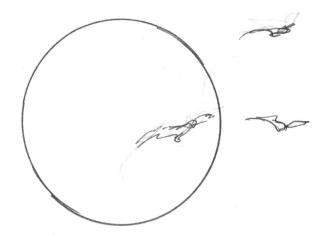
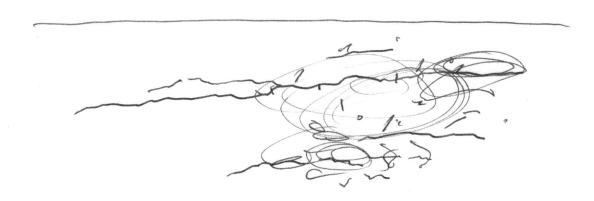

gone, ever near

gone, ever near

Questions. Always questions. Now we have one,
    our turn to ask; to cast:
        when will our nets be filled?
          Our curiosity do still.

"Yours not to know," comes the reply
    as He prepares to ascend on high.
"For now you are to be a witness; that your business.
    Baptize. Teach; the whole world to reach."

Gone. Lifted up on high into the sky.
    Beyond our sight; filled with fright.
Frozen in our upward gaze;
    locked in a fog, a kind of haze.

Suddenly in our midst out of the mist,
    comes the call to move on; now He's gone.
Yet the Advocate to come will guide our way as we stay;
    to do His will, our fears to still.

Come, Oh Holy Spirit, flame of courage,
    light of truth, transform us at the root of our being,
        confirm our believing, strengthen us for preaching,
        guide our witnessing.

Send us forth through doors of fear;
    oh Holy Spirit, be ever near.

Acts, Chapters 1 and 2, p. 74

awake?

awake?

Must have dozed off.
What a dream.
Back to the day's routine.
Can't explain; don't feel the same;
loss is gain; a new game.

Telephone is ringing; a rush of feelings.
Slow to answer; dare I answer?
Dare I not?
Hello…Oh no!
Oh yes.
It's for your best.

Acts 4:5-21, p. 78

Biblical References

All scriptures are from *The New Jerusalem Bible*, 1985.

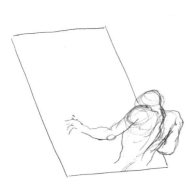

The first four disciples are called
Matthew 4:18-22 ———————————

As he was walking by the Lake of Galilee he saw two brothers, Simon who was called Peter, and his brother Andrew; they were making a cast into the lake with their net, for they were fishermen. And he said to them, 'Come after me and I will make you fishers of people.' And at once they left their nets and followed him.

Going on from there he saw another pair of brothers, James son of Zebedee and his brother John; they were in their boat with the father Zebedee, mending their nets, and he called them. And at once leaving the boat and their father, they followed him.

the call, p. 1

The first four disciples are called
Mark 1:16-20 ———————————

As he was walking along by the Lake of Galilee he saw Simon and Simon's brother Andrew casting a net in the lake – for they were fishermen. And Jesus said to them, 'Come after me and I will make you into fishers of people.' And at once they left their nets and followed him.

Going on a little further, he saw James son of Zebedee and his brother John; they too were in their boat, mending the nets. At once he called them and, leaving their father Zebedee in the boat with the men he employed, they went after him.

wake-up!, p. 3

The first disciples
John 1:35-51

The next day as John stood there again with two of his disciples, Jesus went past and John looked towards him and said, 'Look, there is the lamb of God.' And the two disciples heard what he said and followed Jesus. Jesus turned round, saw them following and said, 'What do you want?' They answer, 'Rabbi' – which means Teacher – 'where do you live? He replied, 'Come and see;' so they went and saw where he lived, and stayed with him that day. It was about the tenth hour.

One of these two who became followers of Jesus after hearing what John had said was Andrew, the brother of Simon Peter. The first thing Andrew did was to find his brother and say to him, 'We have found the Messiah' – which means the Christ – and he took Simon to Jesus. Jesus looked at him and said, 'You are Simon son of John; you are to be called Cephas' – which means Rock.

The next day, after Jesus had decided to leave for Galilee, he met Philip and said, 'Follow me.' Philip came from the same town, Bethsaida, as Andrew and Peter. Philip found Nathanael and said to him, 'We have found him of whom Moses in the Law and the prophets wrote, Jesus son of Joseph, from Nazareth. Nathanael said to him, 'From Nazareth? Can anything good come from that place?' Philip replied, 'Come and see.' When Jesus saw Nathanael coming he said of him, 'There, truly, is an Israelite in whom there is no deception. Nathanael asked, 'How do you know me?' Jesus replied, 'Before Philip came to call you, I saw you under the fig tree. Nathanael answered, 'Rabbi, you are the Son of God, you are the king of Israel.' Jesus replied, 'You believe that just because I said I saw you under the fig tree. You are going to see greater things than that.' And then he added, 'In all truth I tell you, you will see heaven open and the angels of God ascending and descending over the Son of man.'

surrender, p. 5

A visit to Nazareth
Mark 6:1-6 ————————————

Leaving that district, he went to his home town, and his disciples accompanied him. With the coming of the Sabbath he began teaching in the synagogue, and most of them were astonished when they heard him. They said, 'Where did the man get all this? What is this wisdom that has been granted him, and these miracles that are worked through him? This is the carpenter, surely, the son of Mary, the brother of James and Joset and Jude and Simon? His sisters, too, are they not here with us?' And they would not accept him. And Jesus said to them, 'A prophet is despised only in his own country, among his own relations and in his own house' and he could work no miracle there, except that he cured a few sick people by laying his hands on them. He was amazed at their lack of faith.

homecoming, p. 7

The call of Matthew
Matthew 9:9-13 ————————————

As Jesus was walking on from there he saw a man named Matthew sitting at the tax office, and he said to him, 'Follow me.' And he got up and followed him.

- Eating with sinners -

Now while he was at table in the house it happened that a number of tax collectors and sinners came to sit at the table with Jesus and his disciples When the Pharisees saw this, they said to his disciples, 'Why does your master eat with tax collectors and sinners?' When he heard this he replied, 'It is not the healthy who need the doctor, but the sick. Go and learn the meaning of the words: Mercy is what pleases me, not sacrifice. And indeed I came to call not the upright, but sinners.'

bad company, p. 9

The appointment of the twelve
Mark 3:13-19 _____

He now went up onto the mountain and summoned those he wanted. So they came to him and he appointed twelve; they were to be his companions and to be sent out to proclaim the message, with power to drive out devils. And so he appointed the Twelve, Simon to whom he gave the name Peter, James the son of Zebedee and John the brother of James, to whom he gave the name Boanerges or 'Sons of Thunder'; Andrew, Philip, Bartholomew, Matthew, Thomas, James the son of Alphaeus, Thaddaeus, Simon the Zealot and Judas Iscariot, the man who was to betray him.

suspicion, p. 11

The wedding at Cana
John 2:1-12 _____

On the third day there was a wedding at Cana in Galilee. The mother of Jesus was there, and Jesus and his disciples had also been invited. And they ran out of wine, since the wine provided for the feast had all been used, and the mother of Jesus said to him, 'They have no wine.' Jesus said, 'Woman, what do you want from me? My hour has not come yet.' His mother said to the servants, 'Do whatever he tells you.' There were six stone water jars standing there, meant for the ablutions that are customary among the Jews: each could hold twenty or thirty gallons. Jesus said to the servants, 'Fill the jars with water,' and they filled them to the brim. Then he said to them, 'Draw some out now and take it to the president of the feast.' They did this; the president tasted the water, and it had turned into wine. Having no idea where it came from – though the servants who had drawn the water knew – the president of the feast called the bride-groom and said, 'Everyone serves good wine first and the worse wine when the guests are well wined; but you have kept the best wine till now.'

This was the first of Jesus' signs: it was at Cana in Galilee. He revealed his glory, and his disciples believed in him. After this he went down to Capernaum with his mother and his brothers and his disciples, but they stayed there only a few days.

wedding, p. 13

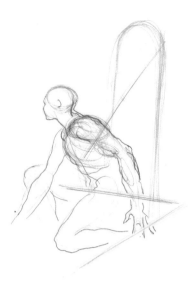

The cleansing of the temple
John 2:13-25 _____

In the Temple he found people selling cattle and sheep and doves, and the money changers sitting there. Making a whip out of cord, he drove them all out of the Temple, sheep and cattle as well, scattered the money changers' coins, knocked their tables over and said to the dove sellers, 'Take all this out of here and stop using my Father's house as a market.' Then his disciples remembered the words of scripture: I am eaten up with zeal for your house. The Jews intervened and said, 'What sign can you show us that you should act like this?' Jesus answered, 'Destroy this Temple, and in three days I will raise it up.' The Jews replied, 'It has taken forty-six years to build this Temple: are you going to raise it up again in three days?' But he was speaking of the Temple that was his body, and when Jesus rose from the dead, his disciples remembered that he had said this, and they believed the scripture and what he had said.

temple, p. 15

The proclamation of John the Baptist
Luke 3:1-20 _____

In the fifteenth year of Tiberius Caesar's reign, when Pontius Pilate was governor of Judaea, Herod tetrarch of Galilee, his brother Philip tetrarch of the territories of Ituraea and Trachonitis, Lysanias tetrarch of Abilene, and while the high-priesthood was held by Annas and Caiaphas, the word of God came to John the son of Zechariah, in the desert. He went through the whole Jordan area proclaiming a baptism of repentance for the forgiveness of sins, as it is written in the book of the sayings of Isaiah the prophet:

A voice of one that cries in the desert:
Prepare a way for the Lord,
make his paths straight!
Let every valley be filled in,
every mountain and hill be levelled,
winding ways be straightened
and rough roads made smooth,
and all humanity will see the salvation
of God.

He said, therefore, to the crowds who came to be baptized by him.. 'Brood of vipers, who warned you to flee from the coming retribution? Produce fruit in keeping with repentance, and do not start telling yourselves, "We have Abraham as our father, " because, I tell you,

God can raise children for Abraham from these stones. Yes, even now the axe is being laid to the root of the trees, so that any tree failing to produce good fruit will be cut down and thrown on the fire.'

When all the people asked him, 'What must we do, then?' he answered, 'Anyone who has two tunics must share with the one who has none, and anyone with something to eat must do the same.' There were tax collectors, too, who came for baptism, and these said to him, 'Master, what must we do?' He said to them, 'Exact no more than the appointed rate.' Some soldiers asked him in their turn, 'What about us? What must we do?' He said to them, 'No intimidation! No extortion! Be content with your pay!'

A feeling of expectancy had grown among the people, who were beginning to wonder whether John might be the Christ, so John declared before them all, 'I baptize you with water, but someone is coming, who is more powerful than me, and I am not fit to undo the strap of his sandals; he will baptize you with the Holy Spirit and fire. His winnowing -fan is in his hand, to clear his threshing-floor and to gather the wheat into his barn; but the chaff he will burn in a fire that will never go out.' And he proclaimed the good news to the people with many other exhortations too.

– John the Baptist imprisoned –

But Herod the tetrarch, censured by John for his relations with his brother's wife Herodias and for all the other crimes he had committed, added a further crime to all the rest by shutting John up in prison.

the end?, p. 17

Peter's profession of faith; his pre-eminence
Matthew 16:13-20

When Jesus came to the region of Caesarea Philippi he put this question to his disciples, 'Who do people say the Son of man is?' And they said, 'Some say John the Baptist, some Elijah, and others Jeremiah or one of the prophets.' 'But you,' he said, 'who do you say I am?' Then Simon Peter spoke up and said, 'You re the Christ, the Son of the living God.' Jesus replied, 'Simon son of Jonah, you are a blessed man! Because it was no human agency that revealed this to you but my Father in heaven. So I now say to you: You are Peter and on this rock I will build my community. And the gates of the underworld can never overpower it. I will give you the keys of the kingdom of Heaven: whatever you bind on earth will be bound in heaven; whatever you loose on earth will be loosed in heaven.' Then he gave the disciples strict orders not to say to anyone that he was the Christ.

identity, p. 19

The transfiguration
Matthew 17:1-8

Six days later, Jesus took with him Peter and James and his brother John and led them up a high mountain by themselves. There in their presence he was transfigured: his face shone like the sun and his clothes became as dazzling as light. And suddenly Moses and Elijah appeared to them; they were talking with him. Then Peter spoke to Jesus. 'Lord,' he said, 'it is wonderful for us to be here; if you want me to, I will make three shelters here, one for you, one for Moses and one for Elijah.' He was still speaking when suddenly a bright cloud covered them with shadow, and suddenly from the cloud there came a voice which said, 'This is my Son, the Beloved; he enjoys my favour. Listen to him.' When they heard this, the disciples fell on their faces, overcome with fear. But Jesus came up and touched them, saying, 'Stand up, do not be afraid.' And when they raised their eyes they saw no one but Jesus.

dis(trans)figuration, p. 21

The resurrection of Lazarus
John 11:1-44

There was a man named Lazarus of Bethany, the village of Mary and her sister, Martha, and he was ill. It was the same Mary, the sister of the sick man Lazarus, who anointed the Lord with ointment and wiped his feet with her hair. The sisters sent this message to Jesus, 'Lord, the man you love is ill. On receiving the message, Jesus said, 'This sickness will not end in death, but it is for God's glory so that through it the Son of God may be glorified.'

Jesus loved Martha and her sister and Lazarus, yet when he heard that he was ill he stayed where he was for two more days before saying to the disciples, 'Let us go back to Judaea.' This disciples said, 'Rabbi, it is not long since the Jews were trying to stone you; are you going back there again?' Jesus replied:

> Are there not twelve hours in the day?
> No one who walks in the daytime stumbles,
> having the light of this world to see by;
> anyone who walks around at night stumbles,
> having no light as a guide.

He said that and then added, 'Our friend Lazarus is at rest; I am going to wake him.' The disciples said to him, 'Lord, if he is at rest he will be saved.' Jesus was speaking of the death of Lazarus, but they thought that by 'rest' he meant 'sleep'; so Jesus put it plainly, 'Lazarus is dead; and for your sake I am glad I was not there because now will believe. But let us go to him. Then Thomas – known as the Twin – said to the other disciples, 'Let us also go to die with him.'

On arriving, Jesus found that Lazarus had been in the tomb for four days already. Bethany is only about two miles from Jerusalem, and many Jews had come to Martha and Mary to comfort them about their brother. When Martha heard that Jesus was coming she went to meet him. Mary remained sitting in the house. Martha said to Jesus, 'Lord, if you had been here, my brother would not have died, but even now I know that God will grant whatever you ask of him. Jesus said to her, 'Your brother will rise again.' Martha said, 'I know he will rise again at the resurrection on the last day.' Jesus said:

> I am the resurrection.
> Anyone who believes in me, even thought
> that person dies, will live,
> and whoever lives and believes in me
> will never die.
> Do you believe this?

'Yes, Lord,' she said, 'I believe that you are the Christ, the Son of God, the one who was to come into this world.'

When she had said this, she went and called her sister Mary, saying in a low voice, 'The Master is here and wants to see you.' Hearing this, Mary got up quickly and went to him. Jesus had not yet come into the village; he was still at the place where Martha had met him. When the Jews who were in the house comforting Mary saw her get up so quickly and go out, they followed her, thinking that he was going to the tomb to weep there.

Mary went to Jesus, and as soon as she saw him she threw herself at this feet, saying, 'Lord, if you had been here, my brother would not have died.' At the sight of her tears, and those of the Jews who had come with her, Jesus was greatly distressed, and with a profound sigh he said, 'Where have you put him?' They said, 'Lord, come and see.' Jesus wept; and the Jews said, 'See how much he loved him!' But there were some who remarked, 'He opened the eyes of the blind man. Could he not have prevented this man's death?' Sighing again, Jesus reached the tomb: it was a cave with a stone to close the opening. Jesus said, 'Take the stone away.' Martha, the dead man's sister, said to him, 'Lord, by now he will smell; this is the fourth day since he died.' Jesus replied, 'Have I not told you that if you believe you will see the glory of God?' So they took the stone away. Then Jesus lifted up his eyes and said:

> Father, I thank you for hearing my prayer.
> I myself knew that you hear me always.
> but I speak
> for the sake of all these who are standing
> around me, so that they may believe it as you
> who sent me.

When he had said this, he cried in a loud voice, 'Lazarus, come out!' The dead man came out, his feet and hands bound with strips of material, and a cloth over his face. Jesus said to them, 'Unbind him, let him go free.'

delay, p. 23

The Messiah enters Jerusalem
Luke 19:28-40

When he had said this he went on ahead, going up to Jerusalem. Now it happened that when he was near Bethphage and Bethany, close by the Mount of Olives as it is called, he sent two of the disciples, saying, 'Go to the village opposite, and as you enter it you will find a tethered colt that no one has ever yet ridden. Untie it and bring it here. If anyone asks you, "Why are you untying it?" you are to say this, "The Master needs it."' The messengers went off and found everything just as he had told them. As they were untying the colt, its owners said, 'Why are you untying it?' and they answered, 'The Master needs it.'

So they took the colt to Jesus and, throwing their cloaks on its back, they lifted Jesus on to it. As he moved off, they spread their cloaks in the road,, and now, as he was approaching the downward slope of the Mount of Olives, the whole group of disciples joyfully began to praise God at the top of their voices for all the miracles they had seen. They cried out:

Blessed is he who is coming
as King in the name of the Lord!
Peace in heaven
and glory in the highest heavens!

**- Jesus defends his disciples
for acclaiming him -**

Some Pharisees in the crowd said to him, 'Master, reprove your disciples.' but he answered, 'I tell you, if these keep silence, the stones will cry out.'

the crowd, p. 25

The washing of feet
John 13:1-20

Before the festival of the Passover, Jesus, knowing that his hour had come to pass from this world to the Father, having loved those who were his in the world, loved them to the end.

They were at supper, and the devil had already put it into the mind of Judas Iscariot, son of Simon, to betray him. Jesus knew that the Father had put everything into his hands, and that he had come from God and was returning to God, and he got up from table, removed his outer garments and, taking a towel, wrapped it round his waist; he then poured water into a basin and began to wash the disciples' feet and to wipe them with the towel he was wearing.

He came to Simon Peter, who said to him, 'Lord, are you going to wash my feet?' Jesus answered, 'At the moment you do not know what I am doing, but later you will understand.' 'Never!' said Peter, 'You shall never wash my feet.' Jesus replied, 'If I do not wash you, you can have no share with me.' Simon Peter said, 'Well then, Lord, not only my feet, but my hands and my head as well!' Jesus said, 'No one who has had a bath needs washing, such a person is clean all over. You too are clean, though not all of you are. He knew who was going to betray him, and that was why he said, 'though not all of you are'.

When he had washed their feet and put on his outer garments again he went back to the table. 'Do you understand?' he said, 'what I have done to you? You call me Master and Lord, and rightly; so I am. If I, then, the Lord and Master, have washed your feet, you must wash each other's feet. I have given you an example so that you may copy what I have done to you.

In all truth I tell you,
no servant is greater than his master,
no messenger is greater than the one who
sent him.

'Now that you know this, blessed are you if you behave accordingly. I am not speaking about all of you: I know the ones I have chosen; but what scripture says must be fulfilled:

The treachery of Judas foretold
Luke 22:21-23

'He who shares my table
takes advantage of me.
I tell you this now, before it happens,
so that when it does happen
you may believe that I am He.
In all truth I tell you,
whoever welcomes the one I send,
welcomes me,
and whoever welcomes me,
welcomes the one who sent me.'

an example, p. 27

'But look, here with me on the table is the hand of the man who is betraying me. The Son of man is indeed on the path which was decreed, but alas for that man by whom he is betrayed!' And they began to ask one another which of these it could be who was to do this.

morsel, p. 29

The treachery of Judas foretold
John 13:21-31 _____

Having said this, Jesus was deeply disturbed and declared, 'In all truth I tell you ,one of you is going to betray me.' The disciples looked at each other, wondering whom he meant. The disciples Jesus loved was reclining next to Jesus, Simon Peter signed to him and said, 'Ask who it is he means,' so leaning back close to Jesus' chest he said, 'Who is it , Lord?' Jesus answered, 'It is the one to whom I give the piece of break that I dip in the dish.' And when he had dipped the piece of bread he gave it to Judas son of Simon Iscariot. At that instant, after Judas had taken the bread, Satan entered him. Jesus then said, 'What you are going to do, do quickly.' None of the others at table understood why he said this. Since Judas had charge of the common fund, some of them thought Jesus was telling him, 'Buy what we need for the festival,' or telling him to give something to the poor. As soon as Judas had taken the piece of bread he went out. It was night.

- Farewell discourses -

When he had gone, Jesus said:

> Now has the Son of man been glorified,
> and in him God has been glorified...

morsel, p. 29

Peter disowns him
John 18:15-18, 25-27 _____

Simon Peter, with another disciple, followed Jesus. This disciple, who was known to the high priest, went with Jesus into the high priest's palace, but Peter stayed outside the door. So the other disciple, the one known to the high priest, went out, spoke to the door-keeper and brought Peter in. The girl on duty at the door said to Peter, 'Aren't you another of that man's disciples?' He answered, 'I am not.' Now it was cold, and the servants and guards had lit a charcoal fire and were standing there warming themselves; so Peter stood there too, warming himself with the others.

As Simon Peter stood there warming himself, someone said to him, 'Aren't' you another of his disciples?' He denied it saying, 'I am not.' One of the high priest's servants, a relation of the man whose ear Peter had cut off, said, 'Didn't I see you in the garden with him?' Again Peter denied it; and at once a cock crew.

memory, p. 31

Jesus before Pilate
John 18: 28-40

They then led Jesus from the house of Caiaphas to the Praetorium. It was now morning. They did not go into the Praetorium themselves to avoid becoming defiled and unable to eat the Passover. So Pilate came outside to them and said, 'What charge do you bring against this man?' They replied, 'If he were not a criminal, we should not have handed him over to you.' Pilate said, 'Take him yourselves, and try him by your own Law.' The Jews answered, 'We are not allowed to put a man to death.' This was to fulfill the words Jesus had spoken indicating the way he was going to die.

So Pilate went back into the Praetorium and called Jesus to him and asked him, 'Are you the king of the Jews?' Jesus replied, 'Do you ask this of your own accord, or have others said it to you about me?' Pilate answered, 'Am I a Jew? It is your own people and the chief priests who have handed you over to me: what have you done?' Jesus replied, 'Mine is not a kingdom of this world; if my kingdom were of this world, my men would have fought to prevent my being surrendered to the Jews. As it is, my kingdom does not belong here.' Pilate said, 'So, then you are a king?' Jesus answered, 'It is you who say that I am a king. I was born for this, I came into the world for this, to bear witness to

the truth; and all who are on the side of truth listen to my voice.' 'Truth?' said Pilate. 'What is that?' And so saying he went out again to the Jews and said, 'I find no case against him. But according to a custom of yours I should release one prisoner at the Passover; would you like me, then, to release for you the king of the Jews?' At this they shouted, 'Not this man,' they said, 'but Barabbas.' Barabbas was a bandit.

loud silence, p. 33

The way to Calvary
Luke 23:26-32 _____

As they were leading him away they seized on a man, Simon from Cyrene, who was coming in from the country, and made him shoulder the cross and carry it behind Jesus. Large numbers of people followed him, and women too, who mourned and lamented for him. But Jesus turned to them and said, 'Daughters of Jerusalem, do not weep for me; weep rather for yourselves and for your children. For look, the days are surely coming when people will say, "Blessed are those who are barren, the wombs that have never borne children, the breasts that have never suckled!" Then they will begin to say to the mountains, "Fall on us!"; to the hills, "Cover us!" For if this is what is done to green wood, what will be done when the wood is dry?' Now they were also leading out two others, criminals, to be executed with him.

why me?, p. 35

The crucifixion
Luke 23:33-43 _____

When they reached the place called The Skull, there they crucified him and the two criminals, one on his right, the other on his left. Jesus said, 'Father, forgive them; they do not know what they are doing.' Then they cast lots to share out his clothing.

- The crucified Christ is mocked -

The people stayed there watching. As for the leaders, they jeered at him with the words, 'He saved others, let him save himself if he is the Christ of God, the Chosen One.' The soldiers mocked him too, coming up to him, offering him vinegar and saying, 'If you are the king of the Jews, save yourself.' Above him there was an inscription: 'This Is the King of the Jews'.

- The good thief -

One of the criminals hanging there abused him: 'Are you not the Christ? Save yourself and us as well.' But the other spoke up and rebuked him. 'Have you no fear of God at all?' he said. 'You got the same sentence as he did, but in our case we deserved it: we are paying for what we did. But this man has done nothing wrong.' Then he said, 'Jesus, remember me when you come into your kingdom.' He answered him, 'In truth I tell you, today you will be with me in paradise.'

one's own, p. 37

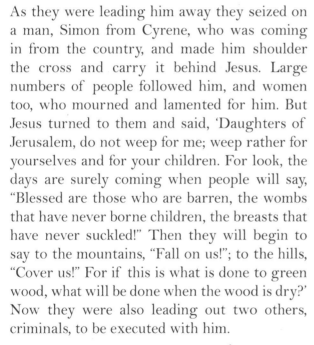

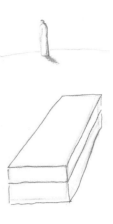

The death of Jesus
Matthew 27:45-56 _____

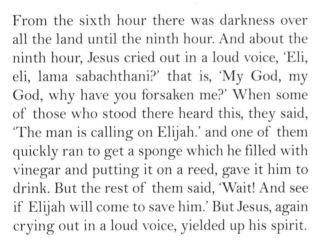

The burial
Mark 15:42-47 _____

From the sixth hour there was darkness over all the land until the ninth hour. And about the ninth hour, Jesus cried out in a loud voice, 'Eli, eli, lama sabachthani?' that is, 'My God, my God, why have you forsaken me?' When some of those who stood there heard this, they said, 'The man is calling on Elijah.' and one of them quickly ran to get a sponge which he filled with vinegar and putting it on a reed, gave it him to drink. But the rest of them said, 'Wait! And see if Elijah will come to save him.' But Jesus, again crying out in a loud voice, yielded up his spirit.

And suddenly, the veil of the Sanctuary was torn in two from top to bottom, the earth quaked, the rocks were split, the tombs opened and the bodies of many holy people rose from the dead, and these, after his resurrection, came out of the tombs, entered the holy city and appeared to a number of people. The centurion, together with the others guarding Jesus, had seen the earthquake and all that was taking place, and they were terrified and said, "In truth this man was son of God.'

And many women were there, watching from a distance, the same women who had followed Jesus from Galilee and looked after him. Among them were Mary of Magdala, Mary the mother of James and Joseph, and the mother of Zebedee's sons.

the UNusual suspects, p. 39

It was now evening, and since it was Preparation Day – that is, the day before the Sabbath – there came Joseph of Arimathaea, a prominent member of the Council, who himself lived in the hope of seeing the kingdom of God, and he boldly went to Pilate and asked for the body of Jesus. Pilate, astonished that he should have died so soon, summoned the centurion and enquired if he had been dead for some time. Having been assured of this by the centurion, he granted the corpse to Joseph who bought a shroud, took Jesus down from the cross, wrapped him in the shroud and laid him in a tomb which had been hewn out of the rock. He then rolled a stone against the entrance to the tomb. Mary of Magdala and Mary the mother of Joset took note of where he was laid.

the tomb, p. 41

The empty tomb, the angel's message
Luke 24:1-12

On the first day of the week, at the first sign of dawn, they went to the tomb with the spices they had prepared. They found that the stone had been rolled away from the tomb, but on entering they could not find the body of the Lord Jesus. As they stood there puzzled about this, two men in brilliant clothes suddenly appeared at their side. Terrified, the women bowed their heads to the ground. But the two said to them, 'Why look among the dead for someone who is alive? He is not here; he has risen. Remember what he told you when he was still in Galilee: that the Son of man was destined to be handed over into the power of sinful men and be crucified, and rise again on the third day.' And they remembered his words.

- The apostles refuse
to believe the women -

And they returned from the tomb and told all this to the Eleven and to all the others. The women were Mary of Magdala, Joanna, and Mary the mother of James. And the other women with them also told the apostles, but this story of theirs seemed pure nonsense, and they did not believe them.

- Peter at the tomb -

Peter, however, went off to the tomb, running. He bent down and looked in and saw the linen cloths but nothing else; he then went back home, amazed at what had happened.

women, p. 43

The road to Emmaus
Luke 24:13-35

Now that very same day, two of them were on their way to a village called Emmaus, seven miles from Jerusalem, and they were talking together about all that had happened. And it happened that as they were talking together and discussing it, Jesus himself came up and walked by their side; but their eyes were prevented from recognising him. He said to them, 'What are all these things that you are discussing as you walk along?' They stopped their faces downcast.

Then one of them, called Cleopas, answered him, 'You must be the only person staying in Jerusalem who does not know the things that have been happening there these last few days.' He asked, 'What things?' They answered, 'All about Jesus of Nazareth, who showed himself a prophet powerful in action and speech before God and the whole people; and how our chief priests and our leaders handed him over to be sentenced to death, and had him crucified. Our own hope had been that he would be the one to set Israel free. And this is not all: two whole days have now gone by since it all happened; and some women from our group have astounded us: they went to the tomb in the early morning, and when they could not find the body, they came back to tell us they had seen a vision of angels who declared he was alive. Some of our friends went to the tomb and found everything exactly as the women had reported, but of him they saw nothing.'

Then he said to them, 'You foolish men! So slow to believe all that the prophets have said! Was it not necessary that the Christ should suffer before entering into his glory?' Then, starting with Moses and going through all the prophets, he explained to them the passages throughout the scriptures that were about himself.

When they drew near to the village to which they were going, he made as if to go on; but they pressed him to stay with them saying, 'It is nearly evening, and the day is almost over.' So he went in to stay with them. Now while he was with them at table, he took the bread and said the blessing; then he broke it and handed it to them. And their eyes were opened and they recognised him; but he had vanished from their sight. Then they said to each other, 'Did not our hearts burn within us as he talked to us on the road and explained the scriptures to us?'

They set out that instant and returned to Jerusalem. There they found the Eleven assembled together with their companions, who said to them, 'The Lord has indeed risen and has appeared to Simon.' Then they told their story of what had happened on the road and how they had recognized him at the breaking of bread.

on the road – again, p. 45

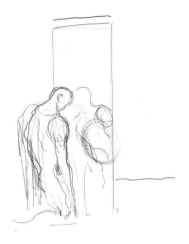

Thomas
John 20:24-29 ─────────────────────

Thomas, called the Twin, who was one of the Twelve, was not with them when Jesus came. So the other disciples said to him, 'We have seen the Lord,' but he answered, 'Unless I can see the holes that the nails made in his hands and can put my finger into the holes they made, and unless I can put my hand into his side, I refuse to believe.' Eight days later the disciples were in the house again and Thomas was with them. The doors were closed, but Jesus came in and stood among them. 'Peace be with you,' he said. Then he spoke to Thomas, 'Put your finger here; look, here are my hands. Give me your hand; put it into my side. Do not be unbelieving any more but believe.' Thomas replied, 'My Lord and my God!' Jesus said to him:

> You believe because you can see me.
> Blessed are those who have not seen and yet believe.

doubting, p. 47

Jesus and Peter
John 21:15-19 ─────────────────────

When they had eaten, Jesus said to Simon Peter, 'Simon son of John, do you love me more than these others do?' He answered, 'Yes, Lord, you know I love you.' Jesus said to him, 'Feed my lambs.' A second time he said to him, 'Simon son of John, do you love me?' He replied, 'Yes, Lord, you know I love you.' Jesus said to him, 'Look after my sheep.' Then he said to him a third time, 'Simon son of John, do you love me?' Peter was hurt that he asked him a third time, 'Do you love me?' and said, 'Lord, you know everything; you know I love you. Jesus said to him, 'Feed my sheep.

> In all truth I tell you,
> when you were young
> you put on your own belt
> and walked where you liked;
> but when you grow old
> you will stretch out your hands,
> and somebody else will put a belt round you
> and take you where you would rather not go.'

In these words he indicated the kind of death by which Peter would give glory to God. After this he said, 'Follow me.'

do you love me?, p. 49

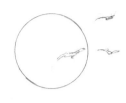

Prologue
Acts, Chapters 1 and 2

In my earlier work, Theophilus, I dealt with everything Jesus had done and taught from the beginning until the day he gave his instructions to the apostles he had chosen through the Holy Spirit, and was taken up to heaven. He had shown himself alive to them after his Passion by many demonstrations: for forty days he had continued to appear to them and tell them about the kingdom of God. While at table with them, he had told them not to leave Jerusalem, but to wait there for what the Father had promised. 'It is', he had said, 'what you have heard me speak about: John baptized with water but, not many days from now, you are going to be baptised with the Holy Spirit.'

- The ascension -

Now having met together, they asked him, 'Lord, has the time come for you to restore the kingdom to Israel?' He replied, 'It is not for you to know times or dates that the Father has decided by his own authority, but you will receive the power of the Holy Spirit which will come on you, and then you will be my witnesses not only in Jerusalem but throughout Judaea and Samaria, and indeed to earth's remotest end.'

As he said this he was lifted up while they looked on, and a cloud took him from their sight. They were still staring into the sky as he went when suddenly two men in white were standing beside them and they said, 'Why are you Galileans standing here looking into the sky? This Jesus who has been taken up from you into heaven will come back in the same way as you have seen him go to heaven.'

- I: The Church in Jerusalem -

- The group of apostles -

So from the Mount of Olives, as it is called, they went back to Jerusalem, a short distance away, no more than a Sabbath walk; and when they reached the city they went to the upper room where they were staying; there were Peter and John, James and Andrew, Philip and Thomas, Bartholomew and Matthew, James son of Alphaeus and Simon the Zealot, and Jude son of James. With one heart all these joined constantly in prayer, together with some women, including Mary the mother of Jesus, and with his brothers.

- Judas is replaced -

One day Peter stood up to speak to the brothers – there were about a hundred and twenty people in the congregation, 'Brothers, 'he said, 'the passage of scripture had to be fulfilled in which the Holy Spirit, speaking through David, foretells the fate of Judas, who acted as guide to the men who arrested Jesus – after being one of our number and sharing our ministry. As you know, he bought a plot of land with the money he was paid for his crime. He fell headlong and burst open, and all his entrails poured out. Everybody in Jerusalem heard about it and the plot came to be called "Bloody Acre", in their language Hakeldama. Now in the Book of Psalms it says:

> Reduce his encampment to ruin
> and leave his tent unoccupied.

And again:

> Let someone else take over his office.

'Out of the men who have been with us the whole time that the Lord Jesus was living with us, from the time when John was baptising until the day when he was taken up from us – one must be appointed to serve with us as a witness to his resurrection.'

Having nominated two candidates, Joseph known as Barsabbas, whose surname was Justus, and Matthias, they prayed, 'Lord, you can read everyone's heart; show us therefore which of these two you have chosen to take over this ministry and apostolate, which Judas abandoned to go to his proper place.' They then drew lots for them, and as the lot fell to Matthias, he was listed as one of the twelve apostles.

- Pentecost -

When Pentecost day came round, they had all met together, when suddenly there came from heaven a sound as of a violent wind which filled the entire house in which they were sitting: and there appeared to them tongues as of fire; these separated and came to rest on the head of each of them. They were all filled with the Holy Spirit and began to speak different languages as the Spirit gave them power to express themselves.

Now there were devout men living in Jerusalem from every nation under heaven, and at this sound they all assembled, and each one was bewildered to hear these men speaking his own language. They were amazed and astonished. 'Surely,' they said, 'all these men speaking are Galileans? How does it happen that each of us hears them in his own native language? Parthians, Medes and Elamites; people from Mesopotamia, Judaea and Cappadocia, Pontus and Asia, Phrygia and Pamphylia, Egypt and the parts of Libya round Cyrene; residents of Rome – Jews and proselytes alike – Cretans and Arabs; we hear them preaching in our own language about the marvels of God.' Everyone was amazed and perplexed; they asked one another what it all meant. Some, however, laughed it off. 'They have been drinking too much new wine,' they said.

– Peter's address to the crowd –

Then Peter stood up with the Eleven and addressed them in a loud voice:
'Men of Judaea, and all you who live in Jerusalem, make no mistake about this, but listen carefully to what I say. These men are not drunk, as you imagine; why, it is only the third hour of the day. On the contrary, this is what the prophet was saying:

In the last days – the Lord declares –
I shall pour out my Spirit on all humanity.
Your sons and daughters shall prophesy,
your young people shall see visions,
your old people dream dreams.
Even on the slaves, men and women,
shall I pour out my Spirit.
I will show these portents in the sky above
and signs on the earth below.
The sun will be turned into darkness
and the moon into blood
before the day of the Lord comes,
that great and terrible Day.
And all who call on the name of the Lord
will be saved.

'Men of Israel, listen to what I am going to say: Jesus the Nazarene was a man commended to you by God by the miracles and portents and signs that God worked through him when he was among you, as you know. This man, who was put into your power by the deliberate intention and foreknowledge of God, you took and had crucified and killed by men outside the Law. But God raised him to life, freeing him from the pangs of Hades; for it was impossible for him to be held in its power since, as David says of him:

I kept the Lord before my sight always,
for with him at my right hand nothing can
shake me.
So my heart rejoiced
my tongue delighted;
my body, too, will rest secure,
for you will not abandon me to Hades
or allow your holy one to see corruption.
You have taught me the way of life,
you will fill me with joy in your presence.

'Brothers, no one can deny that the patriarch David himself is dead and buried: his tomb is still with us. But since he was a prophet, and knew that God had sworn him an oath to make one of his descendants succeed him on the throne, he spoke with foreknowledge about the resurrection of the Christ; he is the one who was not abandoned to Hades, and whose body did not see corruption. God raised this man Jesus to life, and of that we are all witnesses. Now raised to the heights by God's right hand, he has received from the Father the Holy Spirit, who was promised, and what you see and hear is the outpouring of that Spirit. For David himself never went up to heaven, but yet he said:

The Lord declared to my Lord,
take your seat at my right hand,
till I have made your enemies
your footstool.

'For this reason the whole House of Israel can be certain that the Lord and Christ whom God has made is this Jesus whom you crucified.'

- The first conversion -

Hearing this, they were cut to the heart and said to Peter and the other apostles, 'What are we to do, brothers?' 'You must repent,' Peter answered, 'and every one of you must be baptised in the name of Jesus Christ for the forgiveness of your sins, and you will receive the gift of the Holy Spirit. The promise that was made is for you and your children, and for all those who are far away, for all those whom the Lord our God is calling to himself.' He spoke to them for a long time using many other arguments, and he urged them, 'Save yourselves from this perverse generation.' They accepted what he said and were baptised. That very day about three thousand were added to their number.

- The early Christian community -

These remained faithful to the teaching of the apostles, to the brotherhood, to the breaking of bread and to the prayers.

And everyone was filled with awe; the apostles worked many signs and miracles.

And all who shared the faith owned everything in common; they sold their goods and possessions and distributed the proceeds among themselves according to what each one needed.

Each day, with one heart, they regularly went to the Temple but met in their houses for the breaking of bread; they shared their food gladly and generously; they praised God and were looked up to by everyone. Day by day the Lord added to their community those destined to be saved.

gone, ever near, p. 51

Peter and John before the Sanhedrin
Acts 4:5-21

It happened that the next day the rulers, elders and scribes held a meeting in Jerusalem with Annas the high priest, Caiaphas, Jonathan, Alexander and all the members of the high-priestly families. They made the prisoners stand in the middle and began to interrogate them, 'By what power, and by whose name have you men done this?' Then Peter, filled with the Holy Spirit, addressed them, 'Rulers of the people, and elders! If you are questioning us today about an act of kindness to a cripple and asking us how he was healed, you must know, all of you, and the whole people of Israel, that it is by the name of Jesus Christ the Nazarene, whom you crucified, and God raised from the dead, by this name and by no other that this man stands before you cured. This is the stone which you, the builders, rejected but which has become the cornerstone. Only in him is there salvation; for of all the names in the world given to men, this is the only one by which we can be saved.'

They were astonished at the fearlessness shown by Peter and John, considering that they were uneducated laymen; and they recognised them as associates of Jesus; but when they saw the man who had been cured standing by their side, they could find no answer. So they ordered them to stand outside while the Sanhedrin had a private discussion. 'What are we going to do with these men?' they asked. 'It is obvious to everybody in Jerusalem that a notable miracle has been worked through them, and we cannot deny it. But to stop the whole thing spreading any further among the people, let us threaten them against ever speaking to anyone in this name again.'

So they called them in and gave them a warning on no account to make statements or to teach in the name of Jesus. But Peter and John retorted, 'You must judge whether in God's eyes it is right to listen to you and not to God. We cannot stop proclaiming what we have seen and heard.' The court repeated the threats and then released them; they could not think of any way to punish them, since all the people were giving glory to God for what had happened.

awake?, p. 53

William F. Maestri

WILLIAM F. MAESTRI

 A Catholic priest of the Archdiocese of New Orleans, Fr. Maestri resided at the Cathedral of Christ the King in Atlanta, Georgia, in 2008-'09 while he taught at the John Marshall School of Law. He teaches at Notre Dame Seminary Graduate School of Theology in New Orleans. He has authored more than 40 books in the areas of law, ethics and religion.

- *From Virtue to Beatitude: A Journey Through Lent*, 2005
- *Rachel's Dream*, 2004
- *Figures Around the Crib*, 2001
- *Figures Around the Cross*, 2001
- *Word in Season*, 2000
- *Portraits of Extraordinary Women*, 1997
- *Do Not Lose Hope: Healing the Wounded Heart of Women Who Have Had Abortions*, 1987
- *My Rosary Journal: The Great Mysteries*, 1993
- *My Way of the Cross Journal: A Lenten Journey with Jesus*, 1993
- *My Advent Journal*, 1990
- *Paul's Pastoral Vision: Pastoral Letters for a Pastoral Church Today*, 1989
- *Mary: Model of Justice*, 1987
- *Choose Life and Not Death: A Primer on Abortion, Euthanasia and Suicide*, 1986
- *Living Securely within Security*, 1986
- *What Do You Seek?*, 1986
- *Bioethics*, 1983
- *A Priest To Turn To: Biblical and Pastoral Reflections on the Priesthood*, 1983
- *Time for Peace: Biblical Meditations for Advent*, 1983
- *A Time To Be (Re)born: A Biblical Journey Through Lent*, 1982
- *The God for Everyday*, 1981

ROSSIN

Born in Bulgaria, Rossin graduated from Sofia Fine Art Academy. Since coming to the United States in 2001, he has created more than 350 portraits, including two living U.S. presidents and other heads of state. Rossin lives in Atlanta, Georgia, with his wife and two children.

- *President George Bush with President George H.W. Bush*
- *President Obasinjo of Nigeria*
- *U.S. Attorney General, Judge Griffin Bell*
- *Lebanese Patriarch, Vatican, Rome Italy*
- *President Zhelev of Bulgaria*
- *President Klerides of the Republic of Cyprus*
- *Ambassador Andrew Young*
- *U.S. Senator Saxby Chambliss*
- *U.S. Senator Paul Coverdell*
- *Mr. Arthur Blank, Co-Founder, The Home Depot*
- *Mr. Roberto Goizueta, CEO, The Coca-Cola Company*
- *Professor Archibald Cox, Harvard Law School*
- *Miss America, Neevra Jane Langley Fickling*
- *Mrs. Ginger Sullivan, founder, Friends of Morehouse School of Medicine*
- *President William Underwood, Mercer University*
- *Robert L. Steed, King & Spalding Attorney*

Rossin and Fr. Maestri
visit in Rossin's Atlanta studio.
Photo by Guy D'Alema.

Publisher
Éditions du Signe
B.P. 94
67038 Strasbourg - France
Tel: 011 333 88 78 91 91
Fax: 011 333 88 78 91 99
Email: info@editionsdusigne.fr

Author
William F. Maestri

Artist
Rossin

Publishing Director
Christian Riehl

Director of Publication
Joëlle Bernhard

Publishing Assistant
Marc de Jong

Layout
Anthony Kinné - 108405

Credit
From THE NEW JERUSALEM BIBLE, edited by
Henry Wansbrough, copyright © 1985 by Doubleday, a
division of Random House, Inc. and Darton, Longman
& Todd, Ltd. Used by permission of Doubleday, a
division of Random House, Inc.